ANIMAL ODYSSEYS

THE REMARKABLE FLIGHT OF THE MONARCHS

Lynn M. Stone

THE ROURKE CORPORATION, INC.

Vero Beach, FL 32964

Photo Credits:

© Lynn M. Stone: all photos except pages noted.
© Jerry Hennen: 24.
© Becky and Gary Vestal: 29, 33, 37, 39, 42.

Library of Congress Cataloging in Publication Data

Stone, Lynn M.
    The remarkable flight of the monarchs / by Lynn M. Stone
        p. cm. – (Animal odysseys)
    Includes index.
    Summary: Describes the life cycle and amazing migratory flight of the monarch butterfly.
    ISBN 0-86593-108-9
    1. Monarch butterfly – Juvenile literature.
2. Monarch butterfly – Migration – Juvenile literature.
[1. Monarch butterfly. 2. Butterflies.] I. Title.
II. Series: Stone, Lynn M. Animal odysseys.
QL561.D3S76 1991
595.78'9–dc20

                              90-46575
                                   CIP
                                   AC

C O N T E N T S

1 THE MONARCH

The animal world is full of mysterious and exciting journeys. The huge elephant seal finds its way across hundreds of miles of open Pacific Ocean and beaches itself each winter on slivers of sand in Mexico and California. Wildebeest **migrate** by the hundreds of thousands in a thunderous march across the plains of East Africa. Adult salmon leave the ocean and miraculously return to the distant freshwater streams where they were born. Birds have fascinating journeys, too, seasonal **migrations** from north to south each fall and back to northern nesting grounds each spring. But in the entire animal kingdom, perhaps no journey is more remarkable than the flight of the monarch butterflies.

Nearly everyone in the United States has been struck by the beauty of this familiar insect. Making its daily rounds of local meadows and flower gardens, the dazzling black-and-orange monarch is indeed hard to miss. But more impressive than the monarch's beauty are the tales of its passage from egg to adulthood and its amazing **odysseys**.

Imagine for a moment a monarch, born in Maine, that becomes an adult in mid-August. It has about three months to fly south and reach a destination in the rugged mountains of central Mexico. The haven in Mexico will provide it with ideal winter survival conditions. But there is a big catch: the winter retreat is 2,500 miles away. And there is an even bigger catch: none of the millions of monarchs who will be flying to the tiny, mountainous winter site has ever been there before.

If the Maine monarch were a bird instead of a butterfly, it would have a leader. The flock elders would know the route. But although the monarch is about to make a birdlike migration, it doesn't have the birds' leadership or the power of their wings. The monarch is a large, palm-sized butterfly, as many as five inches across, yet it may weigh just one-fiftieth of an ounce. It would take 800 monarchs to weigh a pound! Nevertheless, unlike any other butterfly or insect, the monarch undertakes a truly remarkable journey. The fall migration is massive, joined by tens of millions of monarchs that reached adulthood in late summer.

Not all monarchs fly to the mountains of Mexico on their autumn odyssey. The monarchs of North America are divided into two basic populations, western and eastern. The populations live throughout most of the United States and north into southern British Columbia and Ontario, Canada. They are separated, however, into two populations by the Rocky Mountains, which form the continent's spine, and the desertlike Great Basin region of the West. The western monarchs fly to California while the eastern monarchs, a much larger group, fly to Mexico. Monarchs are also found in Central America and northern South America.

Above: *Monarch caterpillars are often collected and raised on milkweed leaves.*

The mysterious migration of the monarch is only one of the fascinating chapters of its life history. The monarch has long been the favorite butterfly of children and young people because it is easy to find, and its eggs and caterpillars can be collected and "raised" on milkweed plants. Probably no other insect's **metamorphosis** – its development from egg to adult – has been observed more often than the monarch's. And once it has become a free-flying adult, the monarch is still an object of great curiosity – for its beauty and also for its poison. Of course, monarchs don't bite, and the only victims of their poison are the birds that sometimes eat them.

The monarch's diet of bitter milkweed laces its system with substances that are extremely distasteful and often poisonous to birds. Scientists believe that the monarch's wings, boldly splashed in orange, white, and black, help make them easily recognizable as creatures to be avoided.

7

2
A GRAND INSECT

It is hard to imagine the grand, colorful monarch having family ties with mosquitoes, ants, and cockroaches. If appearances and impressions were the measure of an animal's family ties, we might lump butterflies together with other animals whose beauty and flight dazzle us, like swans and eagles. The monarch and many of its butterfly kin seem too colorful and birdlike to be the insects they are. They don't crawl, sting, or show up as unwanted guests on picnic plates. But however grand and glorious they are, butterflies are truly insects.

The monarch and other butterflies are, in fact, quite typical insects. They have an insect's three main body parts – head, thorax, and abdomen. The adult monarch's antennae, eyes, and **proboscis** are parts of its head. The proboscis is a long, coiled tube that the monarch can extend. Through the proboscis it sucks water and plant **nectar**, a nourishing liquid.

Right:
A monarch with its built-in "straw," a black, retractable proboscis, probes a New England aster.

Each of the three thorax sections has one pair of five-jointed legs. The two pair of wings, another typical insect feature, are also on the thorax. The abdomen contains many of the butterfly's internal organs.

Within the insect tribe, butterflies belong to a smaller group known as the **lepidoptera**, or lepidopterans. *Lepidoptera* has its roots in Greek words that mean "one with scaly wings." You can't see them without a microscope, but tiny, intricate scales cover the wings of butterflies and moths, which are also lepidopterans. Over 120,000 **species**, or kinds, of lepidopterans have been identified world-wide. Ten thousand, including the monarch *(Danaus plexippus)*, live in North America.

Left:
Moths like the polyphemus belong to the lepidopterans, just as butterflies do.

If you handle a moth or butterfly, some of the scales from the insect's wings will rub off like colored powder and stain your fingers. Those scales help distinguish moths and butterflies from all other insects.

Just as various large groups of insects have characteristics that separate them from each other, so, too, do moths and butterflies. A butterfly, for example, flies by day; most moths are active at night, and they are attracted to lights. Butterflies have slender antennae with clublike tips, while moth antennae are feathery.

Below:
The monarch's antennae are slim and club-tipped.

11

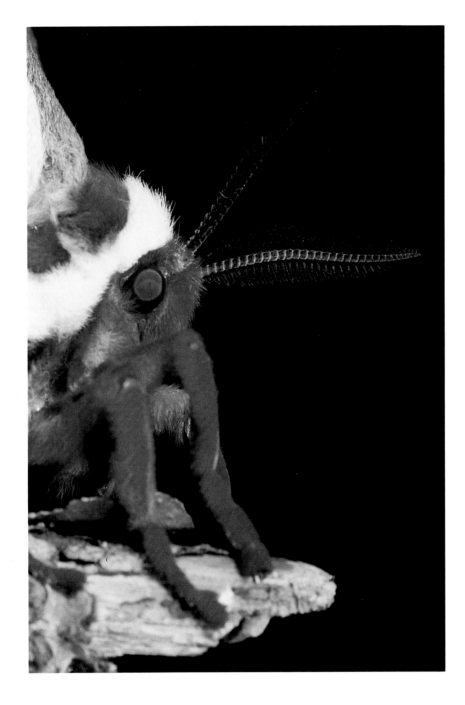

Left:
The cecropia moth's antennae, typical of moths, are feathery, and the moth's body is "furry."

Right:
The queen butterfly of the southern United States is, like the monarch, a "milkweed butterfly."

Moths have plumper bodies than butterflies, and their bodies appear furry. At rest, moths open their wings and butterflies close them over their backs. Other differences between moths and butterflies can be found in their wing structure and in their development in the **pupa** stage of life, which you will read more about later.

Naturally, not all butterflies are alike, any more than all insects or all lepidopterans are alike. The monarch belongs to a family of nearly 60 butterflies that are generally found only in warm places, the world's tropics. Of this group, only the monarch and the smaller, browner queen butterfly are commonly found north of Mexico, and the queen is limited to southern states. Both of these species of butterflies are called "milkweed butterflies." As caterpillars they grow by gobbling up milkweed leaves.

3
PREDATOR AND PREY

The monarch's life history is closely linked to the milkweed. Milkweeds are named for the thick, milky-white sap that flows through their stems and leaves. When a milkweed plant is cut or broken, the sap oozes out. Milkweed plants and their bitter sap are not food for everyone in the insect world. Monarch caterpillars, however, eat virtually nothing else. Over 100 species of milkweed grow in North America, and approximately 2,000 more grow in the tropical corners of the world.

Milkweed provides the growing caterpillar with **nutrition**, food substances that nourish the caterpillar. Nutrition is a normal expectation in an animal's food, but the milkweed plant provides a bonus – a chemical defense. Milkweed contains poisons. Although they don't affect monarchs, these poisons affect many animals, so the milkweed is generally ignored by animals. Among the few exceptions, along with the monarch, are the queen butterfly, milkweed bugs, and the milkweed leaf beetle.

Above:

Milkweed fuels the monarch caterpillars and also provides a chemical defense.

The monarch benefits from the milkweed's poison by storing it in its body. The monarch does not have poison sacs like a rattlesnake; the milkweed poisons simply become part of its flesh. The monarch thus makes itself poisonous to an animal that eats it. Even though an adult monarch does not eat milkweed, it keeps the poison that it consumed as a caterpillar.

The monarch's chief natural **predators** – the animals that hunt and eat it – are certain birds. A bird does not know that the monarch is poisonous until it tastes one. Sometimes a bird bites into a monarch and, noticing the bitter taste, spits it out. On other occasions, the bird's experience is even more unpleasant. If the bird swallows a monarch, the butterfly poison may cause the bird to throw up. One experience with a mouthful of orange-and-black butterfly is usually enough. The bird does not chase monarchs for its **prey** again.

The viceroy butterfly apparently profits from the monarch's natural defense. Viceroys are slightly smaller than monarchs and belong to a different group of butterflies, but they look remarkably like monarchs. Although viceroys do not contain milkweed poisons, birds seem to avoid them because they look like monarchs. This type of defense, in which one animal resembles another, is called **mimicry**.

The monarch's defense does have its flaws. Milkweeds do not all contain the same level of poison. Consequently, the level of poison in monarchs varies. Monarchs that grow up eating some species of milkweed are far more distasteful than monarchs that grow up on others. Birds that happen to find monarchs with low levels of milkweed poison in their systems are likely to continue hunting them. In a study of monarchs that wintered in California, about half were poisonous enough to make birds throw up.

Studying monarchs at a wintering site in Mexico, scientist Dr. Lincoln Brower and his students made a startling discovery. They found that two kinds of birds, orioles and grosbeaks, were killing 35,000 monarchs each day. Like detectives, the scientists set about finding out why the monarchs were not making these birds miserably sick.

Milkweed poison in monarchs can be read almost like fingerprints. A scientist can tell what kind of milkweed the monarch ate by analyzing samples from the butterfly. The scientist may also have a fair idea of where the monarch fed, based upon where certain milkweed species live. Dr. Brower found that the Mexican monarchs he was studying had eaten a common milkweed that is only mildly poisonous. And because the species grows readily on land that has been plowed or otherwise disturbed, it has become increasingly abundant. The possibility exists that as more monarchs feed on this particular milkweed, they will become more frequent prey for birds.

Left:
This swamp-loving milkweed in northern Illinois is one of over 100 milkweed species on which monarchs dine in North America.

Birds are not the only monarch predator. During the winter, monarchs are quite inactive in the cool weather. Sometimes they are blown from their roosting trees onto the ground. If the air is cold enough, the monarchs cannot fly; they have to wait on the ground until the weather warms and makes them active. During these cool spells, grounded monarchs may be eaten by mice, shrews, ants, and even cattle. Feeding monarchs sometimes fall prey to spiders after becoming entangled in their webs.

Above:
Occasionally a monarch falls prey to a spider, like the familiar black and yellow argiope.

Right:
A monarch probes iron-weed for nectar.

Monarch butterflies themselves live on a liquid diet of nectar and water. Some of the nectar is drawn from milkweed blossoms, but monarchs visit dozens of flower species – New England asters, goldenrod, ragweed, false foxglove, and sunflowers among them. A monarch feeds by sucking liquid through its long proboscis. While the butterfly settles onto a flower's blossoms and balances itself by pumping its wings, its proboscis probes deep into the flower center for nectar.

The monarch, in fulfilling its own need for nectar, unwittingly fulfills one of the plant's needs at the same time. By flying from flower to flower, the butterfly picks up and transfers tiny grains of **pollen** powder. Without this transfer of pollen from flower to flower, many plants could not produce seeds.

4
FROM EGG TO ADULT

Most of our familiar animals look much like their parents even when they are born. As they grow, they increase in size and perhaps change color. The famous "ugly duckling" in Hans Christian Andersen's story grew up to be a swan because it was, of course, a swan all the time. Even as a "duckling" it had two eyes, two little wings, a bill, feathers, webbed feet, and the shape of a miniature swan. It wasn't really ugly; it just didn't look like the other ducklings. Similarly, a kitten is a miniature version of a cat.

In the world of insects, development into adulthood follows a much stranger path. The monarch undergoes what scientists call a complete metamorphosis, or change. Only when a monarch is an adult, at the final stage of the metamorphosis, does it look like a butterfly. Prior to adulthood it passes through three stages of development. None of them hints at the bright, broad-winged insect that will finally result.

A monarch begins life as a tiny, bullet-shaped egg attached to the underside of a milkweed leaf. It is critical that the female monarch choose a milkweed for her egg because the insect's next stage will have to feed on milkweed. Each female may lay 300 to 400 eggs. An egg may take as few as three days to hatch or as many as 12. Cool weather slows the egg's development, and warm weather speeds it along.

What hatches from the monarch egg is not a miniature monarch butterfly. Rather, it is the monarch's **larva** stage, a tiny caterpillar with the appetite of a lumberjack. For the next two weeks the caterpillar prowls milkweed plants. Using its jaws to cut the leaves, it stuffs itself on one leaf after another. Its growth rate is startling, and it has to shed its skin four times to make room for its growing body. Its weight actually increases 2,700 times. If a six-pound human baby matched the monarch caterpillar's rate of growth for two weeks, it would weigh as much as a bull elephant – about eight tons!

At the end of the larval stage, the greenish caterpillar is about two inches long. It looks like a gift-wrapped sausage, candy striped in orange, black, and white. As a full-grown caterpillar, the monarch begins the pupa stage of its development. This is a resting period for the monarch after its active life as a hungry caterpillar.

The caterpillar, soon to be a pupa, attaches itself to a leaf or stem by means of a tiny silk "button" that it spins with its mouth onto the plant. The button is the

Left:
*A monarch
caterpillar
attaches itself
to a leaf and,
in a J posture,
begins to
transform into
a pupa.*

Left:
*Some moth
caterpillars,
such as the
cecropia, spin
a silk cocoon
and spend the
winter as a
pupa inside the
cocoon.*

extent of the monarch caterpillar's weaving. Moths, not butterflies, spin silk cocoons in which they live as pupas.

The monarch pupa is also known as a **chrysalis**. The monarch's chrysalis stage lasts about two weeks. During its first few days, the chrysalis is a distinctive milky green with specks of gold. It looks less like a butterfly at this stage of development than the caterpillar did. Later, as the monarch pupa becomes more of a butterfly, the outer layer of the chrysalis becomes increasingly blue and transparent. Like an envelope of plastic wrap, the chrysalis reveals in growing detail and color the black veins and orange wings of the adult butterfly.

The monarch reaches its full development after its two weeks in the pupa stage. It then breaks free of the chrysalis shell. The new butterfly is rumpled, like an old glove that has been stuffed into a pocket. But for two weeks the monarch has scarcely moved, and it is patient now as it emerges. The monarch is in no condition to flex its wings and sail away. It rests and uncoils its long, tubular body. Its wings are soft and look like pleats of crushed velvet. The monarch expands its wings by

Below left:
The monarch chrysalis is milky green with flecks of black and gold.

Below right:
As the butterfly develops, the pupa shell becomes more revealing.

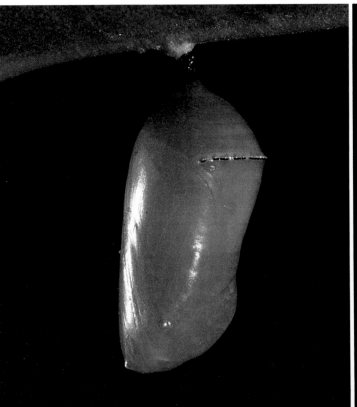

pumping clear green liquid into them. Within a few
hours the wings dry and stiffen. Now the monarch, in
the fourth and final stage of its metamorphosis, flutters
away to satisfy its craving for nectar and water. It will
not have a problem finding flowers. Its instincts and its
senses of smell, sight, and taste are sure guides to nec-
tar-rich flowers.

The days of sweeping over meadows and marshes
and sipping nectar from wildflower bouquets are brief.
The monarch's odyssey from egg to butterfly took about
five weeks. As an adult, the monarch will live only a few
weeks or at the most a few months. Early summer
monarchs spend themselves in the heat, flying, feeding,
courting, and reproducing their kind. Their colors fade
and their wings begin to tatter like shopworn paper.
After only two or three weeks, they die. But for the
monarchs born in late summer, life takes a different
twist.

Right:
The monarch rests after emerging from the chrysalis and dries its wings.

5 THE REMARKABLE FLIGHT OF THE MONARCHS

In late summer the hours of sunlight decrease and the nights cool, giving rise to early mornings draped in mist. Now and then the threat of frost hangs in the wind. Changes in nature's rhythm do not pass unnoticed by the summer's last generation of monarchs. The butterflies feel an urgency to leave their birthplaces where cold weather is approaching. Previous monarchs of the season traveled too, but not the incredible distances that the August and September monarchs will go.

The late summer monarchs are just one of several generations of monarch born during the summer months. When monarchs fly north from Mexico in the spring, they lay eggs immediately in southern and southwestern states. Most of the egg-laying adults and their mates die there, but when their eggs develop into butterflies some five weeks later, they continue the species' flight north. It is too hot to dally and produce another generation of monarchs in the South, at least in large numbers. These monarchs, like their parents who spent the winter in Mexico, soon also die, but they carry the migration of monarchs a few hundred more miles. And so through the warm months, the migration of the eastern monarchs leapfrogs northward, finally stalling in Canada.

It is unlikely that any of the butterflies born the preceding August survive for a full year and reproduce where they were born. At best, an elderly monarch probably lives no more than eight months.

Each new generation of monarchs moves the species gradually northward. By August the first signs of autumn ripple across the North. In the generation of monarchs born in late summer, internal changes in their bodies take place. These monarchs receive and process a different "message" than the monarchs who lived earlier in the summer. Subtle changes in the length of daylight and cooler weather trigger different behavior in these late summer monarchs. Unlike their immediate ancestors, these monarchs have no desire to spend their energy on reproducing their own kind, nor do they have the desire to head north. Rather, their energies are devoted to increasing their reserves of fat, called **lipids**, and flying south.

Lipids come indirectly from the nectar that monarchs drink. Nectar contains sugar that the butterflies convert into fat, their source of energy. The light, airy

Left:
Late summer monarchs increase their fat reserves, which will be used in migration, by drinking nectar.

wings and the muscles that power them wouldn't be of any service without the lipid fuel to drive them.

Large flocks of monarchs begin to gather and move southward in August and September. North winds and approaching cold fronts prompt mass movements of the butterflies, especially on the coasts and in the Great Lakes area. If conditions are good, monarchs can fly up to 200 miles in a day. If conditions are difficult, the monarchs may not fly at all – or they may fly and be blown astray. Monarchs have been storm-tossed as far as Great Britain and an island in the South Pacific, 4,000 miles from the United States.

Various species of butterflies have devised different ways of surviving winter. Many are immune to the cold in one or another of their developmental stages. The monarchs' answer to cold – mass migration – is unique among butterflies. No one knows with certainty how long the monarchs have made their long migrations. They probably began at least 10,000 years ago when the **glaciers**, giant rivers of ice, retreated and the Earth's climate warmed. The monarchs presumably spread northward to follow the expanding range of the milkweed. When winters arrived, however, the monarchs

Below:
Migrating monarchs roost in trees and shrubs.

were forced to retreat south or freeze. Being butterflies of the tropics, they had no way of surviving long periods of cold in any of their four life stages.

Once the migration has begun, the monarchs travel south by day and rest at night. They roost in trees and shrubs, often in great clusters. Many a home owner has been pleasantly surprised to find migrating monarchs clustered onto trees in the yard. When the morning sun warms them, they flutter into fields and gardens, gorging themselves with nectar and flying south with the wind.

Their journey is quite unhurried. Monarchs are strong fliers by butterfly standards, but they probably cannot fly over 25 or 30 miles per hour. More often they probably cruise along at about 10 miles per hour. The wind influences their flight speed considerably.

Just how high monarchs sail over ground level is a matter of some debate. They are often at the mercy of wind currents. At times they may travel at a height of one kilometer, about 3,000 feet.

During their migration the monarchs are battered by wind, rain, and occasional hail. Their flights take them over mountains, cities, and scores of highways and rails. That tens of millions of these insects survive the flight is astounding. But even more remarkable is the distance that some of them fly. According to Dr. Brower, the monarchs that winter in Mexico traveled an average of 1,800 miles on their fall flight. Those from Maine and southern Canada flew 2,500 to 3,000 miles! Scientists can't attach radio collars to monarchs and track their journeys as they would a bear's or coyote's. But Dr. Fred Urquhart, a Canadian **entomologist**, or insect scientist, helped pioneer the tracking of monarchs by tags. He and others have marked thousands of monarchs with small, sticky wing tags.

Tagging has helped to solve questions about which monarchs migrate to which wintering sites. It cannot solve the most perplexing question of monarch migration: How do monarchs find their way? Remember that most of the monarchs traveling south in the fall are accurately directed toward isolated patches of forest in California or in the mountains of central Mexico. Remember too that none of the monarchs has ever seen its winter destination before. The monarchs seem to follow an invisible path or current. As Dr. Brower says, "Nobody has yet discovered what guides these tiny, fragile creatures on the long journey."

6
BRANCHES OF BUTTERFLIES

Whatever the mysterious force that guides the monarchs on their remarkable flight is, it works with uncanny accuracy. Almost the entire eastern population of monarchs that survives migration settles each November into one of some 30 known winter colonies in Mexico. All of the Mexican colonies discovered thus far have been in a small section of the Sierra Madre Mountains. It is a region just 75 miles long and 35 miles wide in the states of Michoacan and Mexico. The area is between 9,000 and 11,000 feet above sea level near the city of Zitacuaro, about 75 miles west of Mexico City. Here, on the moist, wooded mountain slopes, some 200 million monarch butterflies gather each November. Their colonies are as small as one-tenth of an acre and as large as 10 acres.

The monarchs cover branches, trunks, and leaves. The upper parts of the trees appear to be draped with loose, dull orange shingles. On warm days, legions of monarchs bask on woodland paths and fly in grand clouds. The concentrations of the butterflies are breath-

Right:
On moist, wooded slopes in the mountains west of Mexico City, monarchs gather by the millions.

taking. Imagine as many as four million monarchs on one acre of land!

The western monarchs settle into sheltered groves of woodland along the California coast. The most famous of these colonies is at Pacific Grove on the Monterey Peninsula. California's wintering monarchs arrive from as far north as southern British Columbia. Others come from Oregon, Washington, and various parts of California. Estimates of the California wintering population vary from 10 million to 40 million.

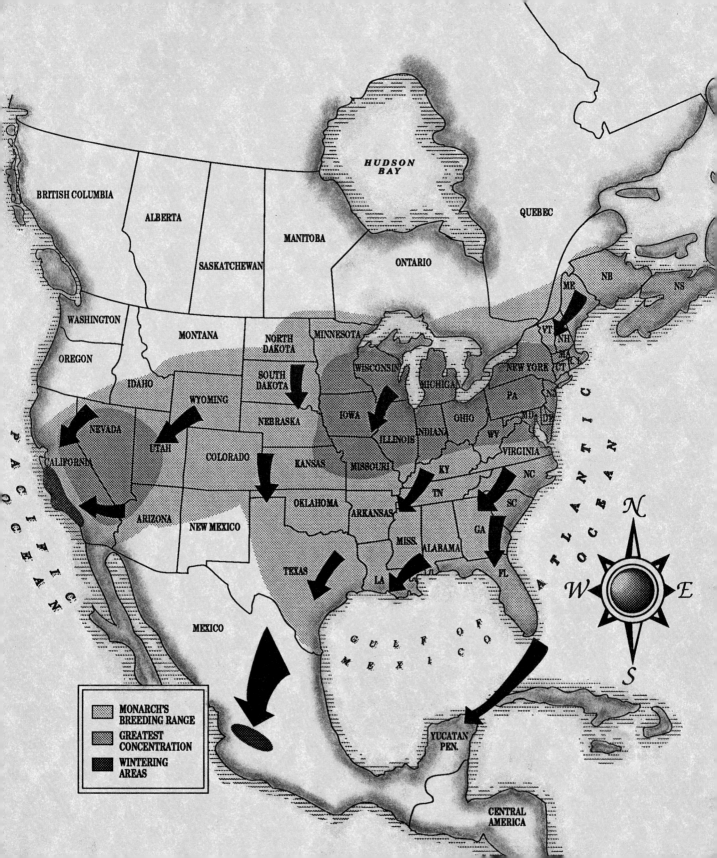

A few wintering colonies of eastern monarchs are located on the upper gulf coast of Florida. Why these eastern monarchs do not winter in Mexico as their relatives do is not clear. One theory is that monarchs without proper fat reserves – the ragtags in the flocks – remain in Florida rather than continuing their journey. Presumably others in the flocks that migrate into Florida continue on to Mexico. If the theory that weak butterflies drop out is correct, it is a wise decision. Otherwise, the monarchs might face an impossible task – flying across the Gulf of Mexico to Texas or Mexico.

For many years, scientists did not think that monarchs made long flights over open sea, at least not by choice. But reports of monarchs in staggering numbers landing on oil drilling rigs in the Gulf of Mexico has forced a closer look at migration patterns. Apparently the monarchs that sweep onto oil rigs are attempting to reach the Mexican wintering sites. How many others take the sea route and how many are successful in making an ocean crossing are questions as yet unanswered.

While Mexican colonies aren't the monarchs' only wintering grounds, they are certainly the most spectacular – and the most difficult to reach. Until recently, no one knew where the mountain colonies were except for the people who lived nearby. Although Mexican farmers and villagers knew the colonies' whereabouts, scientists did not know of their existence until 1975. Dr. Urquhart had studied the monarchs' movements for years. He felt certain that they wintered in central Mexico, but he did not know where. Dr. Urquhart wrote to Mexican newspapers in an effort to enlist the help of local people in finding the wintering sites. Ken Brugger, who lived in Mexico City, offered his assistance. With the aid of his wife, Brugger found a colony in January, 1975, and notified Dr. Urquhart. Several colonies have been discovered since, all in the same general area as the first.

The California and Mexico winter sites share a similar climate – moist and cool. Pacific winds laden with humidity keep the levels of temperature and moisture fairly steady. Florida weather is less stable. Heavy, killing frosts and unseasonably hot weather are both factors in causing the Florida roosts to be less permanent and long-lasting than the roosts in California and Mexico.

Moisture is important to wintering monarchs. Moist air helps the butterflies keep their body moisture. Without the moist air to breath and from which to take water, the monarchs would be in constant search of nectar and water. By being able to absorb moisture from the air, the monarchs don't have to fly to sources of moisture as often. During the winter, flights burn valuable energy from fat reserves that cannot be easily replaced. Although wildflowers and their nectar are fairly

abundant in November, they begin to disappear as the season advances.

Ideally, wintering monarchs burn as little energy as possible. They are in a state much like refrigeration. Their body functions are slowed down and they are generally inactive. Like flowers kept in a refrigerator, their lifespan is increased and their freshness is kept intact during the cool months. The butterflies rest quietly in clusters much of the time, but their relaxed state is nothing like the deep sleep which some animals experience to pass the winter away. In Mexico, the monarchs squeeze onto firs, cedars, pines, and some broad-leaved trees. On warm, sunny days, the heat stirs them into flight. When millions of butterflies become airborne, the groves whisper with the sound of their wings.

These wintertime flights are short. The monarchs settle onto sunlit paths to bask or fly off in search of water at a spring or brook. On particularly hot days, they may fly simply to rid themselves of heat. Resting in the sun causes a faster loss of stored energy than flying does. If clouds intercept the sun, the monarchs quickly return to their roosting trees. Wintering monarchs are very sensitive to changes in air temperature, Dr. Brower and his students have learned.

The minimum temperature at which a monarch can fly with some ease is 55°F. At this temperature, a monarch's wing muscles are warm enough to give the insect a quick lift-off. Temperatures below 55°F can spell trouble, for a monarch that is flightless is also helpless. Freezing temperatures can be even more troubling. James Anderson, one of Dr. Brower's students, learned that some monarchs will die if the air temperature dips even slightly below freezing (32°F). If the air temperature drops to 18°F, half of the monarchs will die. A tempera-

ture of 10°F will kill all of the monarchs. On a chilled night in January, 1981, one of the Mexican colonies lost at least two and one-half million monarchs when the temperature plunged to 25°F.

Forest growth is an important feature of monarch winter sites, partly because of its relationship to temperature. Like a blanket, the forest helps trap enough

Left: *Protection for monarchs wintering in the great colonies of Mexico has not been secured.*

depend upon farming for a living and upon trees for heat and cooking. Monarca has been showing local people how to earn a living from the cleared land that they already have. The farmers have been encouraged to plant orchards, raise fish, and build greenhouses. Many of the mountain villagers have been guiding thousands of tourists to the butterfly colonies and selling monarch art. But not all Mexicans are willing to change their lifestyles to protect butterflies in the woods. Some people feel that the Mexican government, which announced its support for the monarch sites, has done little to enforce its protective laws.

But what can, or should, the government do? Should it force poor people to stop harvesting firewood and burning hillsides to make room for little farms?

Right:
Warm, sunny days spark brief flights of wintering monarchs in the Mexican colonies.

ture of 10°F will kill all of the monarchs. On a chilled night in January, 1981, one of the Mexican colonies lost at least two and one-half million monarchs when the temperature plunged to 25°F.

Forest growth is an important feature of monarch winter sites, partly because of its relationship to temperature. Like a blanket, the forest helps trap enough heat to keep night temperatures from becoming too cold. During the day, it provides shade. It also protects monarchs from gusty winds, rain, hail, and occasional snow.

In March the wintering monarchs of Mexico and California undergo internal changes, again triggered by the changes in weather and the longer periods of daylight. The monarchs are no longer in a refrigerated state. They are overwhelmed by the urge to mate and fly northward. The lack of activity has slowed their aging process by about four months. Now they are restless and single-minded in their determination to leave the mountains. They head north, a winged carnival of orange and black. Much of their energy is burned in courtship chases. A male flies after the female and woos her with scent that he carries on his hindwings. Eventually, the female deposits a series of eggs, scattering them on milkweed plants over many miles.

The monarchs lay their eggs as they spread across northern Mexico and the southern United States. They stop to sample the bright, spring flowers that lie across their path like candies. But the path grows shorter each day and with each passing wingbeat. The remarkable flight is nearly over; the monarchs' bodies are spent. But their eggs and the new sprouts of milkweed have guaranteed the survival of their race. Six months from now a future generation of monarchs will pass this way. They will be southbound for the green, moist mountain forests where there are butterfly trees in the clouds.

7
SAVING THE REMARKABLE FLIGHT

Will there be butterfly trees forever? That is a troublesome question for the monarch's human supporters. Many people and organizations have worked to see that the monarchs will always have a safe haven on their wintering grounds. Without protection of the winter homes, the great flocks of monarchs we now enjoy will no longer exist. The monarch is not **endangered** as a species; it is not in danger of becoming **extinct**. But the spectacular passage of millions upon millions of monarchs in their seasonal flights is endangered as long as the monarchs' winter homes are not secure.

In Mexico, where the greatest number of monarchs idle the winter away, the government granted some protection to monarchs in 1986. Logging and land clearing were banned in and around several of the monarchs' winter roosts. In addition, the World Wildlife Fund and Monarca, a Mexican conservation group, contributed funds and ideas. Many of the mountain people

depend upon farming for a living and upon trees for heat and cooking. Monarca has been showing local people how to earn a living from the cleared land that they already have. The farmers have been encouraged to plant orchards, raise fish, and build greenhouses. Many of the mountain villagers have been guiding thousands of tourists to the butterfly colonies and selling monarch art. But not all Mexicans are willing to change their lifestyles to protect butterflies in the woods. Some people feel that the Mexican government, which announced its support for the monarch sites, has done little to enforce its protective laws.

But what can, or should, the government do? Should it force poor people to stop harvesting firewood and burning hillsides to make room for little farms?

Serious problems in monarch conservation and human welfare still exist in the mountains of Mexico. Each year the forests seem to move farther and farther up the slopes as land is cleared.

Once upon a time the Mazahua Indians of Mexico shook wintering monarchs from their frosty perches. They placed the groggy insects in jars and took them home. Later they fried and ate them, apparently with no ill effects from the milkweed poisons. Frying pans are no longer a threat to the wintering monarchs. But there are other threats, far greater than the Mazahuas' curious tastes.

The human population in Mexico is growing rapidly, and the pressure for land and firewood is great. Even though monarchs may not cluster on every tree in a grove, they are dependent on the entire grove. Trees help keep air temperatures steady, so by thinning a forest, wood cutters cause little changes in air temperature within the grove. The air becomes cooler at night, hotter by day. When a winter storm swirls into the butterfly trees, the loss of even one degree can spell death to the monarchs.

In California, colonies in the state park system are secure. Those outside the parks and in private ownership are in some cases threatened by developers. Monarchs usually winter in groves within a few hundred yards of the Pacific Ocean. Such sites are nearly always as attractive to people as they are to butterflies. In the mid-1980s, at least eight wintering sites were destroyed by the development of homes.

Nevertheless, the residents of California have shown a growing concern for their butterfly trees. In 1988, Californians voted to spend several hundred thousand dollars for the purchase and protection of monarch sites.

Monarchs are not **exotic** insects. They are almost as familiar as your backyard. And because they are so

Left:
Blooming wildflowers, such as those on this scrap of native prairie in Illinois, are a banquet for butterflies.

Right:
Everyone can help preserve monarchs by protecting their environment – and ours.

familiar, you are probably in a position to help secure the monarch's future. Encourage people in your community to stop the spraying and cutting of roadside and railside wildflowers. Blooming wildflowers are a banquet table for monarchs and other butterflies. In your own yard, plant bright flowers and provide places with sun, shade, and shallow water for butterflies. If you plant milkweed for monarchs, be sure it is one of the milkweeds that naturally grows in your area.

You can help preserve the magic of these butterflies. Become involved in activities and organizations that help protect the environment that you share with the monarchs.

45

chrysalis – the pupa; the inactive stage of insect development between larva and adult

endangered – in danger of becoming extinct

entomologist – one who studies insects

exotic – a plant or animal introduced into an environment in which it did not naturally occur

extinct – the state of no longer existing

glacier – a massive river of ice capable of gradually advancing or retreating in accordance with the climate

larva – the caterpillar; the stage of insect development between egg and pupa

lepidoptera – a group of insects with tiny wing scales; the butterflies and moths

lipids – fatty substances

metamorphosis – the process of changes in which an animal, especially an insect or amphibian, develops into an adult

migrate – to make predictable seasonal movements from one location to another

migration – a predictable seasonal movement from one location to another some distance away

mimicry – the similarity of one plant or animal to another of a different kind for the advantage of the mimic

nectar – a sugary liquid produced by plants

nutrition – nourishment

odyssey – a long journey

pollen – powder produced by some plants as a part of their reproduction process

predator – an animal that kills and feeds on other animals

prey – an animal hunted for food by another animal

proboscis – the long, coiled, tubular structure used by a butterfly for drinking nectar

pupa – *see chrysalis*

species – a group of plants or animals whose members naturally reproduce only with other plants or animals of the same group; a particular kind of animal, such as a *monarch* butterfly

Numbers in boldface type refer to photo and illustration pages.

Monarchs are easily observed at one time or another because they live throughout much of North America. They are often abundant in meadows that are rich with wildflowers and milkweeds.

Observing the great, wintering clusters of monarchs is not as simple a task. Despite their broad breeding range, monarchs gather each fall and winter at a relatively few wintering sites, most of them in California and Mexico. Anyone who wishes to see the huge wintering flocks, some of them numbering in the millions, will have to visit California or the isolated mountains west of Mexico City, Mexico. A few smaller flocks of monarchs winter in north Florida.

You might consider observing the monarch's development by collecting a monarch egg on the underside of a milkweed leaf. Or collect a monarch caterpillar, which you can probably find feeding on a milkweed. Once you have a monarch caterpillar, be sure to keep it in an airy but escape-proof container. Also be sure to give it a fresh supply of milkweed. Eventually the caterpillar will develop into its chrysalis stage. Soon after, you should be able to see the adult monarch emerge.

Monarch Sites (Wintering Flocks)

Butterfly Grove Inn and George Washington Park, Pacific Grove, CA

Natural Bridges State Beach, Santa Cruz, CA

North Pismo Beach State Park, CA

Pt. Mugu State Park, CA

Transvolcanic Range in the states of Mexico and Michoacan, Mexico

Ed. Note: Sites listed here do not represent *all* the places where monarchs winter. They do represent sites that are reliable and, in the case of California, have relatively easy access.